THE S CREMATION

BY
TODD W. VAN BECK

When exploring the history of death in general three clear and distinct facts emerge. First is the undisputed, unarguable, and inevitable fact that the death rate globally is a perfect round even one hundred percent – no question about this. This fact is a concern of many but is also in the present age being conveniently ignored by just as many, if not more. Second is the almost undisputed, almost unarguable, and almost inevitable fact that concerning the disposition of dead human bodies two methods have been available to people to dispose of their dead: earth burial and cremation. Third is the almost always unspoken history that human beings have found disposing of their dead both challenging and basically unpleasant, even though there are basically only two choices to be made at the time of death – burn or bury? It is historically interesting that when all is said and done, throughout all the centuries of fiddling with this and changing that, concerning the disposition of our dead in the end basically just two choices are available for most earth people, only two: earth burial and cremation.

To be sure there are wide variations and approaches to earth burial and cremation, for instance there is a farmer in the Midwest of the United States who for a small amount of money will take a sampling of the cremated remains, fill a shot gun shell with a small portion of the cremated remains and blast them into the atmosphere. Then on the other hand there are the unique Towers of Silence where the dead body is left exposed to the air and environment and birds are allowed to devour the corpse and then the birds in turn do the natural thing and deposit remnants of the corpse throughout the countryside, a type of post mortem fertilizer cycle process if you will.

However even with the myriad variations that people throughout history have created to dispose of their dead (and there have been many), still in the end it comes down to two simple choices: burn or bury.

Another consistent theme in exploring the history of dealing with the dead is the abundantly clear fact that living people find dead people problematic, and with good reason. To not properly care for our dead is for most places on earth unkind, unlawful, and unsanitary. Living people have a consistent history of viewing corpses as being problematic.

The question which has confronted every generation since the beginning of time concerning dead people comes down to this: "What should we do with them?" The answers that people throughout history have come up with are fascinating to say the very least, and if we were to explore all the possible answers our task for our purposes here would never come to an end.

The purpose of this work has a specific task which is to explore the history of cremation, but first a few words about the philosophy of history will be helpful.

HISTORY

Many people like, some people even love history, but just possibly only a few loyal purists of history actually like and love the myriad of dates which seem to be connected with every historical account, and which so many people as young people were compelled to memorize in school which proved to be a tortuous experience, with the result that people ended up hating history.

People seem to easily become distracted and even annoyed or worse bored to death when and if too many dates are thrust upon them. It is confusing, and understandably so. Certainly dates have their place, dates are important, but as we will soon see cremation actually started before we had dates or even chronological time for that matter, so instead of a linear work complete with using numerous dates as the overall outline, we use instead the written approach as an historical narrative with a few references to dates tossed in for good measure to keep the purists happy.

This book is a story about cremation, and most people love being told stories on any subject, and the story of cremation is if it is anything is a story about people and how they have approached the issue of using fire to dispose of dead bodies. The best history always comes down in the end to sharing the story.

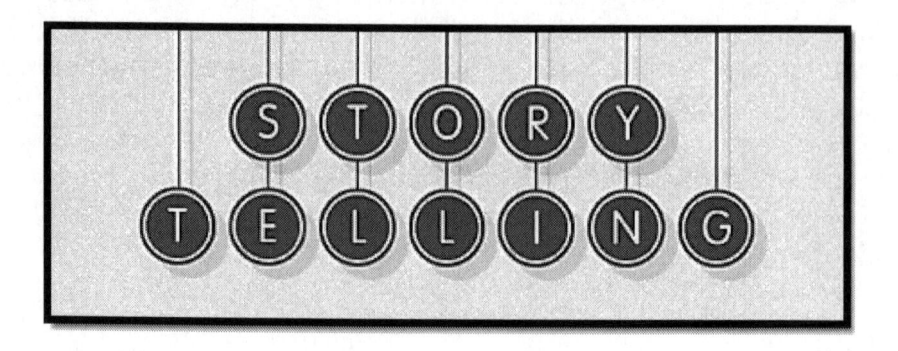

STORY TELLING

However for people who are addicted to dates, and consider the narrative approach to history as being sloppy and heretical this chapter concludes with a historical chronology of the dates that trace the significant events in the history of cremation and is included to satisfy the reader who does like and love dates.

Let's begin.

No human being can live without history. Even people who say they hate history have a history and live in history. If you have a heartbeat you have experienced history and are creating history with every breath you take. In fact while dogs and cats certainly have a history they are most probably not aware of their history in any shape or form, and in any event even if it is proven that they have some primitive glimmer of past events they cannot possibly be as aware of their history as human beings are. Any history concerning the experiences dogs and cats must come from humans for humans are the only creatures on earth that can write down experiences and that are aware of their history, and most importantly have the capacity to learn life lessons from their history and pass these lessons on to others – this is called education.

Everything concerning existence has a history, and it is true that the more people know about their history the more chances they have of increasing their own wisdom and judicious perspectives on the daily task of living life. <u>Winston Churchill</u> was once quoted as saying: "Study history, study history, study history." Churchill's words ring true for our purposes in this part of the book.

While this is not a work concerning an analysis of the philosophy of history a couple of historical insights for the reader will be helpful. First when reading this information it will be valuable to realize the truth of the old adage that history repeats itself. History proves the truth of this well used thought. As we will see in our historical journey concerning cremation there is really nothing new under the sun concerning cremation and what people have done in the past and will do in the future concerning burning dead bodies has a repetitious history with the common denominator being that each and every generation believes their history is unique, that their problems are like the world has never seen before, and that what they do in the present time will affect the global experience for years to come. This sometimes happens in history but such monumental history changing events in reality are very rare. However concerning cremation the most unique and special historical event to happen was simply the ability to generate tremendous amounts of heat, and the type of heat that got hot quickly. This was no easy task as we shall soon see, but to even come close to claiming that anything to do with cremation qualified as a monumental historical event is simply an overstatement, and we do not want to overstate things in this chapter.

The second insight is this: Every generation, most particularly those members of a particular generation who are ignorant or worse disinterested in their history, are most likely compelled to repeat the mistakes of the past. As the great Harvard philosopher <u>George Santayana</u> hauntingly reminds us: <u>"Those who forget their past are condemned to repeat it."</u>

It will be valuable for the reader to keep these two historical analysis points in mind concerning the philosophy of history as this information is explored.

This book is organized into four major headings, and these are not in order of importance. The headings are:
<u>1. SIGNIFICANT EVENTS IN TIME,</u>
<u>2. RELIGIOUS THINKING AS A POWERFUL INFLUENCE,</u>
<u>3. INDUSTRIAL DEVELOPMENTS THAT GENERATED HIGH HEAT</u>
<u>4. THE CULTURAL NUANCES THAT FIDDLES WITH DEATH ATTITUDES.</u>

1. SIGNIFICANT EVENTS IN TIME

There are no records of a time in history when cremation has not been present, and because of this no one really knows where and when the practice began. In other words cremation history first and foremost has no definite beginning, and it certainly has no definite end. If the student of this history looks for primary sources, verifiable documents, or even cave man drawings concerning the genesis of cremation that student is doomed to failure. Cremation is so ancient that much of what has been promoted as historical fact is in truth history based anecdotes, oral traditions, and well-intended speculation.

While our historical verification of the beginnings of cremation is somewhat sketchy what we do have is the story of "The Mungo Lady."

In the late 1960's *Professor Jim Bowler* a geomorphologist with the University of Melbourne (Australia) discovered the fossilized remains of a woman in the Willandra Lakes Region of Lake Mungo, in New South Wales, Australia. Immediately the corpse was dubbed The Mungo Lady. When her remains were carbon dated she was found to have lived approximately 20,000 to 26,000 years ago, making her one of the oldest anatomically-modern humans ever found in Australia and the world.

It was certain that after The Mungo Lady died, her remains were cremated. From burn mark patterns on the bones it was discovered that the Mungo Lady's remains had undergone an unusual ritual for the time – the body was burned, then the bones were partly crushed, and then the cremated remains were burned for a second time. The first cremation probably was botched and did not complete the burning process which was the reason for the second, however another theory has been promoted that possibly her descendants performed this unusual ritual a second time to ensure that she did not return to haunt them, but no matter this is speculation.

Regardless of the well-intended speculations the discovery of The Mungo Lady was extremely important because it represents the world's oldest known cremation.

What is known, however, is that throughout history (until contemporary times) earth burial by far had superseded cremation as the preferred and the most accessible and practical method of taking care of the age old problem of disposing of our dead.

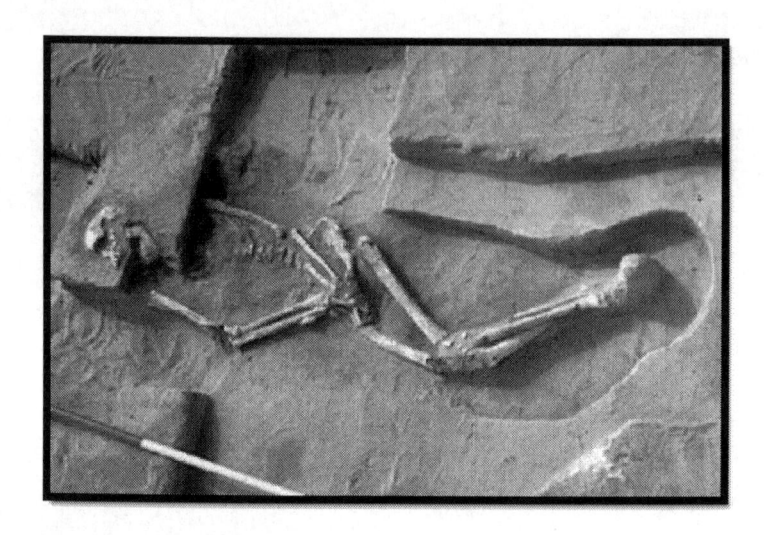

People who are devoted to and make their livelihoods literally digging up history, the archeologists and anthropologists of the world report that cremation most probably started during the Stone Age in the Near East and some places on the European Continent.

One of the simple practical and common sense impediments which tremendously affected the use of cremation was the glaring issue of the consistent inability of these ancient people (and people for a long time to come) to be able to simply generate enough heat to actually burn a dead body thoroughly, and here thoroughly is the key word. One can only speculate just how many "botched" cremations were performed which ended up in a partially burned cadaver, and it does not take much of an imagination to think of ancient people when the cremation was botched, a job half done just throwing their hands up in the air and leaving the offensive scene for nature to take its inevitable course of disposing of the cadaver. It is safe to conclude that a partially cremated dead body would have been just as repugnant and distasteful to our Bronze Age cousins as it is today when the crematory retort malfunctions and literally the flame goes out half way through.

There was also another practical problem for these ancient people concerning cremation. To just survive they needed wood to burn for cooking food, and for heat, not necessarily for burning dead bodies which in any event took a good amount of time, and also a good amount of wood. Wood had other much more important and vital purposes for these people than just the funeral pyre. Wood equaled literal survival.

In the study of ancient cremation history the beginnings of the acceptance of cremation, regardless of available fuel and convenience appear to be rooted in the thinking and philosophies of the Greeks. The Greeks embraced cremation not because of some odd ritual requirement which used fire, but not surprisingly the Greeks based some of their interest in the practice of cremation on the revolutionarily new idea for the time of public health concerns. None other than Plato himself proclaimed that no earth burials (this included cremations) should be made in agricultural fields or by places which were highly populated. It would be a great overstatement to say that the Greeks embraced cremation on the level that we see currently in some places in the world, but it is clear that the Greeks viewed cremation with an acceptance that had not been seen before in history.

The Greeks also, being somewhat aggressive in warfare at times, used cremation as a very practical method of bringing back the bodies of dead Greek warriors who had died gloriously in battle in some far off land. The rationale of course being, easier and much more pleasant to ship a small bundle of cremated remains 2000 miles, without the obnoxiousness of decomposition, than to attempt to ship a corpse 2000 miles that would be in the advanced stages of decomposition upon arrival. The Greeks were also the first to decide that in the instance of cremation you could also have earth burial – simply bury the cremated remains. Here then is a good example of the historical truth that there is nothing new under the sun, for contemporary cremation practices use this method of inurnment burials routinely. People who are illiterate of cremation history might well believe the practice of inurnment is a new idea, and someone out in the present world might even be so bold as to take credit for inventing the inurnment idea, but that would be historically incorrect. The Greeks of antiquity invented the cremation urn burial.

Frequent and protracted battles throughout the ancient classical world made cremation first a commonplace thing, and then for the military anyway the preferred means of disposal of the heroic warrior dead. Although ground burials were used for most everyday Greeks, cremation became so closely associated with valor, manly virtue, patriotism, and military glory that in time it was regarded as the only fitting end to an epic life.

THE GREEK WAR HERO'S CREMATION

Status symbols are not new, and in ancient Greece the greater the glorified and worshipped war hero the higher the cremation conflagration needed to be.   The *Iliad* tells how elaborate and elegant cremation became for Greek heroes. For instance Zeus, the supreme deity, compels the victorious Achilles to turn over the corpse of Hector so that the slain hero's father, King Priam of Troy, can cremate it in royal style. Achilles earlier had ordered a huge funeral pyre built one hundred square feet to gloriously burn to ashes the body of his slain friend Patroclus. Unfortunately nothing lasts forever and sadly after an arrow pierced Achilles all-too-vulnerable heel, the leader of the Trojan War was himself afforded the most spectacular incineration yet – it was a classic case of status, keep up with the Jones' and good old-fashioned one-upmanship.

As the Greeks went, so did the Romans, however the inventive and economically savvy Romans turned cremation into profit or they tried to.   By the time of the great Roman conquests and empire building the idea of extramural burials (outside the city walls) was accepted as being the normal method of disposing of the dead. This is compared to intramural burials where the dead were always buried within the city walls.

<u>Virgil</u> in the *Aeneid* lambasts the tasteless, crude etiquette of cremation conducted without religious funeral rituals and ceremonial fanfare (oh where did the Greeks go?), done merely for profit and expediency (a kind of contemporary immediate disposition Roman style). On the other hand Virgil praises a conflagration in which the correct kinds of dried leaves, twigs, and dead cypresses are set ablaze to the prayerful cries of the mourners who are circling the cremation funeral pyre.

The Romans were quite skilled at putting on elaborate ceremonies, pageants and rituals. Today's New Orleans Mardi gras celebration harkens its beginnings back to the Roman funeral processions of old. The Romans even had their own version of ancient funeral directors that were called <u>*LIBITIANRIUS*</u> and they were in business to organize all type of death activities, which included cremations, and to be paid for their services.

Predicated on all these Greek and Roman cremation activities was this issue of money. The poor of both cultures might well have been cremated, but the poor received communal cremations. The elaborateness of Roman cremations made them life's last status symbol. Whereas the indigent, the poor, the wretched went up in small flickering flames, and usually as a group, the wealthy departed this world in towering infernos, however such cremation opulence was not to last.

It will be helpful here to interject the reminder that cremation, while it is evident throughout history in truth is not the oldest form of disposing of a dead body (earth burial holds that record), and it needs to be clarified that cremation throughout history has always been an example of the merging of and living with the tensions created by the merger of sacred rituals combined with secular customs.

History is never black and white it is a series of transitional grays. At this juncture we need to make the first gray transition by easing from significant events in time to religion as a powerful influence for in the history of cremation significant events and the influence of religion go hand in hand.

2. RELIGION THINKING AS A POWERFUL INFLUENCE:

About one hundred years after the death of Jesus Christ the fires of cremation slowed down considerably and in some places it simply stopped. The cutoff is historically abrupt and only suggestively understood, however two very powerful factors probably contributed to this snuffing out of the cremation fires.

First is a practical explanation. Under the Greek and Roman civilizations world travel changed by increasing with explorations the world over and in order to travel you needed ships, and in order to build ships, and large ships to boot, you needed wood, and a lot of wood, tons of wood.

During the ten decades that followed the death of Jesus Christ the Roman Empire experienced a severe shortage of wood, not because they were building ships but specifically because so many trees had been felled for centuries to fuel their magnificent cremation pyres. However with the new world explorations of the Roman Empire and with wood as being the principal building materials for ships and fortresses and now at a premium price, the Roman government placed severe restrictions on the use of timber and this eventually turned into a ban on the use of wood. Outdoor cremation, anyway the Roman way was, after all, not an activity to be pulled off clandestinely.

Wood in Rome may well have possessed economic and shipping and exploration influence, but by this time another powerful, more powerful than wood influence was happening. It was a new growing religion which also possessed an ever growing political and economic power – it was called Christianity. The spread of Christianity played a tremendous role in the decline of cremation and this fact should not be underestimated. However before an historical exploration of Christian influence on the issue of cremation it will be helpful to begin at the beginning of the origins of Christianity – namely Judaism.

One feature of both Judaism and Christianity are that they are religions that have books. Before the Jewish writings and hence books, most religious activities were a series of random rituals, many times brutal rituals, where everything from a goat, to a bushel of corn, to a human being was offered in sacrifice to the myriad of gods which people worshipped. However, for the most part the rituals and beliefs attached to these "mystery religions" (and there were thousands of them) were not written down. The emergence of Judaism changed all that. Judaism took the world from being polytheistic to being monotheistic, which means from believing in many gods to believing in one God. Today this might strike some as unimportant, but make no mistake this movement proved to be one of, if not the most significant change in world thinking and history since creation.

The great British theologian and mathematician <u>Alfred North Whitehead</u> was once asked at the end of his life what in his opinion were the two greatest events that had happened in history? Lord Whitehead paused for a moment and responded, "The invention of anesthesia, and the elimination of polytheism."

Prior to the wisdom writings found in Jewish religious and sacred texts little importance was placed on or an

14

acknowledgement made concerning the worth of just one human life. Life was cheap. Judaism changed all that. Within the Jewish wisdom teachings and writings the human being was seen as a creation that had worth and most importantly the individual human person was created by the one true God. Hence there emerged from Jewish teachings for the first time in world history an ethical approach of reverence for the sacredness of just one human life, and you did not have to have financial wealth or royalty to qualify as being important in the eyes of God. This religious ethic of the Jews had been unheard of in most all civilizations up to this time, and this Jewish reverence for human life translated quickly into the Jewish teachings concerning reverence for the Jewish dead. For the Jew life and death went hand in hand.

Because of the ethic of reverence for the dead for the ordinary Israelite family death then was a highly significant event. When there was a death a close relative would close the eyes of the deceased. The dead body was then bathed, fully dressed and humbly carried on a wooden bier to the burial site.

Cremation was unheard of, and it is interesting as to just why the Jews discarded cremation, because without question they would have been exposed to the practice in their already long and eventful history.

The early Jewish experience was one of community this was a key to survival. Humility and sharing amongst each other was critical in fact many times this communal practice of helping each, by placing value on others literally translated into survival of the Jews. Because the individual person who was part of the Jewish religious community had special significance, when they died the Jewish community approached the death with quiet reverence, with solemn rituals, with prayers, with the reading of verses from their sacred texts – and also with humility. The death of a member of the community held great religious and social significance.

THE "LEVAYA" – THE JEWISH FUNERAL PROCESSION

The result of this community importance that the Jews placed on both significance and humility appears in historical retrospect to be an unspoken yet by action departure from what the Jews considered to be the paganism, the status symbols, the flash and the pageantry of the Greek and Roman way of death, and the result of this attitude was that the Jews turned their backs away from cremation. Cremation for the early Jew was then a double edged sword being both a total destruction of God's creation, and it was also proud, arrogant and totally lacking in humility. The result the Jew's would not cremate.

Also the Jewish thinking often times viewed fire as being punishment (this view would be adopted by the later Christians).

From Jewish traditions flowed the Christian movement. It is clear that just as Judaism was a religion with books, with teachings, with writings, with sages, with wisdom, so began Christianity as a religion with books – many books. Of primary focus in the Christian movement was the documentation and writing down in books the teaching and sayings of Jesus.

Early Christianity did not explicitly forbid cremation (as the later church would), but it sternly frowned on burning the body of a Christian for two supreme reasons: the Pagans routinely cremated their dead to mock the Christians belief in a bodily resurrection, therefore Christians should not cremate; *and most compelling Jesus had not been cremated.*

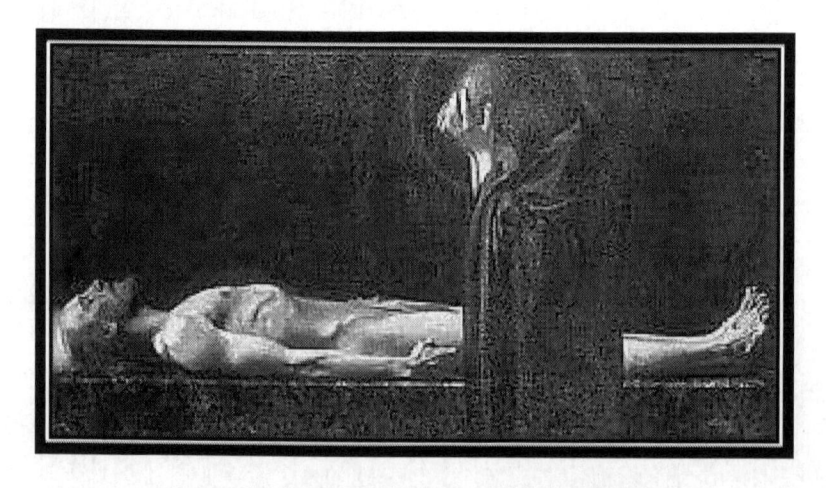

THE ENTOMBMENT OF JESUS CHRIST

In the very earliest days of the Church one of the negative reactions by the Church towards the Roman Empire was that after Christians had been martyred the Roman government would take their bodies, which were viewed as being the Temple of God by the Christians and would incinerate the Martyrs and then have the sacred (to the Christians) remains scattered. The Roman logic being that with this highly visible indignity the Romans could easily declare that there was no way the Christian God could reunite the body and soul of the Martyrs as preached by the early Church. Two results of this Roman insult were the Christian development of the underground Catacombs where their sacred dead would be protected and safe and the growing and rigid prohibition against cremation as a choice for Christians for the final disposition of the body after death.

> **"YOUR BODY IS A TEMPLE OF THE HOLY SPIRIT"**
> 1 CORINTHIANS 6:19

As Christianity grew the leadership of the Church believed firmly that cremation was not a wise decision. Not only did the Christian leaders point to the mockery that Pagans were tossing at them by cremating the Christian and their own dead, they also concluded that the Bible clearly teaches that the body is the Temple of the Holy Spirit and that cremation was hence viewed as completely destroying God's creation, whereas they pointed to earth burial as not being totally and completely destructive. - Also the early Christians pointed to the natural slow processes that earth burial afforded.

It was true that permission could be given to use cremation under "extraordinary" circumstances such as the years of the plague in Europe during the Middle Ages, but as a general rule the early Christians, and later the organized Catholic Church outlawed cremation as an un-Christian act that was in reality a cruel attempt by pagans to disprove the core belief of Christians during this period about the revered and fervent Christian hope of a reunited body and soul at the final Resurrection.

The first governmentally proclaimed prohibition concerning the practice of cremation for Christians came when Constantine the Great, the first world leader of importance to embrace Christianity prohibited cremation everywhere within his realm.

Christianity has a history even to this very day of never truly being at peace with the issue of cremation. However some of the world's religions, such as Hinduism, practice cremation as an essential part of their historic death rituals. However in the historical perspective of the Western civilization, Christianity frowned very much upon cremation which they had inherited as a hold over tenet of Judaism, and both Judaism and Christianity frowned upon cremation because both were actively attempting to abolish Greco-Roman pagan rituals.

Within the Christian framework the religion that has had the most objections to cremation has been the Roman Catholic Church. This prohibition against cremation became so pronounced that in May of 1886 *Pope Leo XIII* promulgated Canon Law #1203 which read: "The bodies of the faithful must be buried, cremation is forbidden." Also within the contents of Canon Law #1203 there was another mandate forbidding Roman Catholics from joining societies whose purpose it was to spread the practice of cremation, because according to the Vatican in 1886 such a membership implied a denial of the resurrection of the body. During the Vatican II council a discussion was started of how to use cremation in a manner that would fit into the Roman Catholic Funeral Rite and allow the human body to be treated with the dignity that it deserves. It had become apparent that many times the use of cremation was following adopted local customs, and was also at times necessary for economic and health reasons. The message was clear: cremation was not being exclusively viewed as anti-Christian anymore.

On May 8, 1963 *Pope Paul VI* removed Canon Law #1203, and throughout the four decades since the cremation rate has risen steadily, for Roman Catholics too.

Regardless of the contemporary acceptance of cremation by many modern Christian bodies it is historic fact that the Christian movement has a strong history of resisting cremation, but nothing lasts forever – historically speaking.

As the strength of the Christian movement gathered force and power there was a concentrated effort to weed out any vestiges of paganism, and certainly the Christians of antiquity associated, and with good reason, the practice of cremation with pagan rituals and their accompanying ridicule. In fact the great Charlemagne of France proclaimed punishment by death for those who performed cremations.

In addition to the churches ever growing power and influence was the clear Christian distinction that Christians liked grave spaces, monuments, tombs, cemeteries and particularly the holy relics of early Christian saints.

Even when the issue of wood consumption was brought up the early Church had a quick response. It was better, they replied, to use wood to construct tombs and monuments than it was to use the combustible material in making cremation pyres. In Westminster Abbey to this day can be seen a magnificent tomb made of solid oak wood in which is entombed Edward the Confessor, and this tomb has lasted intact over many centuries.

Throughout parts of Europe, cremation was strictly forbidden by law, and even punishable by death if combined with pagan and heathen rites. Cremation was even sometimes used by church authorities as part of the punishment for heretics, and this did not only include burning the person alive at the stake.

The Church over time was very successful at associating cremation with a fiery eternal punishment that bordered on clear previews of what an everlasting hell, fire, and damnation would be like. For example so associated had the Church become with the symbol of fire as a powerful tool of the everlasting punishment of hell to instill obedience in the faithful, that in 1428 an astonishing 44 years after his death the Church had the condemned heretic _John Wycliffe's_ (the translator of the Bible from the Latin Vulgate into English) body exhumed and cremated and had his ashes thrown into the River Swift explicitly as a posthumous punishment for the world to see for his prior denials of the truth of the Roman Catholic doctrine of transubstantiation (the doctrine that teaches that in the Eucharist the substance of wheat bread and grape wine changes literally into the substance of the Body and Blood of Jesus). The theological thinking of the Church at the time (1428) being that by burning the bodies of "heretics" like long dead *John Wycliffe* it was hoped that when Christ returned it would be impossible for any heretic like poor old John Wycliffe to be resurrected and reunited with Christ.

Some of the various Protestant denominations came to accept cremation with the theological rationale being, if God can resurrect an entire dead body, then God can just as easily resurrect a bowl of ashes and dust and create a new body. Still the Roman Catholic Church resisted from allowing cremation and in the 1908 Catholic Encyclopedia it referred to the Protestant efforts at justifying cremation as a "sinister movement" and even went as far as associating the advancement of the acceptance of cremation with Freemasonry.

Overall the Christian opposition to cremation lasted for 1500 years.

It was only a matter of time however before certain social forces such as printed books, and the presence of people who knew how to read, and free thinking began to challenge and even start to dismantle the 1500 year old Christian prohibition of cremation.

By 1658 a fellow named *Sir Thomas Browne* authored a book on burial customs, and in this publication he adds an honest and well balanced narrative on cremation, which Sir Thomas approved of and since he held notable power and influence his position concerning cremation was a much needed endorsement, publically anyway.

In 1710 none other than the wife of the Treasurer of Ireland boldly and with great conviction and bravado (for a woman of the time) made known her wishes to be cremated. She based her decision upon her assessment of the horrible condition of most of the Irish churchyards she had examined. Her wish provoked quite an outcry and particularly from the Roman Catholic Church in Ireland, but already the subject of cremation was going full circle.

Then on top of all this chatter about cremation in 1822 the famous English poet *Percy Bysshe Shelley* was drowned in the Mediterranean and according to the Tuscan health laws of the time he was cremated as a protection against the spread of disease. Suddenly the devoted followers of Shelley's poetry quickly converted to requesting cremation for themselves upon their own deaths.

It is time for another history transition into yet another shade of gray – let's take a look at an interesting but little spoken about subject concerning cremation – industrial developments that generated high heat.

3. INDUSTRIAL DEVELOPMENTS THAT GENERATED HIGH HEAT

For all of the rich and substantive history of death care, cremation emerges with one unique requirement which none of the other body disposing activities need nor require, but for cremation is an absolute requirement – heat and a lot of heat.

A grave can easily be dug without using heat. In fact the only time heat is used to dig a grave is in some localities during the middle of winter where the frost is so deep that the ground is heated with propane so the grave can be dug. A funeral can easily be conducted without using fire, and mourning practices rarely use fire, save for the candles here and there in the mortuary, home or church.

Without heat, however there is no possible way to cremate a dead human body. As we have already established obtaining heat in the history of cremation was not only a monumental task, there were no guarantees that once you had heat that it would be enough to get the job done, or that it would last long enough for a complete burn or that you could even get it hot enough.

A brief history of ovens and furnaces here will be helpful, because ovens revolutionized cremation.

Ancient people began cooking on open fires. These cooking fires were placed on the ground and later simple masonry construction was used. By the Middle Age taller brick and mortar hearths often with chimneys were being built. The first written record of an oven being built refers to an oven built in 1490 in Alsace, France, and this oven was made entirely of brick and tile including the flue.

Around 1728 cast iron ovens were being made in quantity, but with the churches prohibition towards cremation during this period few if any people associated ovens with cremations.

By the late 1860's however experiments were being made by a number of independent inventors, particularly in Italy. A certain _Professor Brunetti_ made a big splash of sorts at the Vienna Exposition in 1873 by presenting his new furnace contraption. However these creative inventors were still stymied by the age old challenge of cremating a dead human body; namely generating enough sustained heat to completely incinerate the body. Interestingly furnaces that could melt iron had been invented by this time and were being used, but they were useless in the attempts to cremate a single human being simply because while the individual crematory furnaces seemed unable to generate enough heat, the "blast" furnaces in the iron mills, if used, would create so much heat as to literally vaporize the dead human body and this was not an option.

THE VIENNA EXPOSITION – 1873

However things began to look up for cremation technology when the British inventor _James Sharp_ patented a gas oven in 1826 however the initial operation of the new apparatus was unsuccessful, however by the 1870's the gas oven had been perfected, and gas lights, gas ovens, gas heating sources were being used in millions of homes across the globe.

JAMES SHARP INVENTED THE ABILITY TO GET AND SUSTAIN HIGH HEAT

Around this time there was growing support for cremation in Germany and in England. In England none other than the personal surgeon to Queen Victoria, _Sir Henry Thompson_ inspired the cremation movement in his country. Sir Henry was concerned with the deplorable conditions of the English churchyards, and saw it as a genuine threat to public health. Sir Henry even attended the Vienna Exposition and saw Professor Brunetti's invention and returned to England with a cremation mission set in his mind. He wrote an article in which he favored cremation, and quickly a debate both written and spoken began between Sir Henry and the Church of England (who of course was firmly against cremation), and many in the public who also held strong opinions for and against cremation.

In 1874 Sir Henry formed the Cremation Society of England with a membership comprised of mostly free thinkers, Unitarians, liberals and socialists and people (the newspapers reported) "without any professed religious conviction."

By 1878 the Cremation Society of England erected its first crematory in Woking and used a furnace which clearly generated enough heat for the required time to thoroughly cremate a dead human body. However the growth of the Cremation Society of England was slow going.

THE CREMATION SOCIETY OF ENGLAND

Now enter the eccentric yet highly creative and infamous Dr. William Price of Wales. Dr. Price received much fame and attention for his deep involvement with a revival of the Druid religious movement in his native country. Dr. Price today is recognized as one of the most unusual people in Victorian Britain. For all Dr. Price's eccentricities and he had many; for instance he would not wear socks because he thought them unhygienic, and he wore a large fur hat on his head and dressed in bright green coats covered with bright red buttons, and he thought that he had been specifically chosen by a Druid god to deliver the Welsh people from bondage from Great Britain. Also Dr. Price did not believe in marriage, as he proclaimed it as enslavement of a woman, but he himself was interestingly married twice.

DR. WILLIAM PRICE – CREMATION ADVOCATE AND DRUID

    However it was Dr. Price's stance on cremation that both got him into trouble, but also made him a cremation hero in Great Britain and changed the course of cremation in that country forever. Here is the story.

    In 1883 Dr. Price had a son born who he named "Iesu Grist" (Welsh for Jesus Christ). The young infant died five months later, and Dr. Price believing that burying a corpse polluted the earth decided to cremate his son. When Dr. Price himself started the cremation pyre many townspeople noticed the fire and when they found out that Dr. Price was trying to cremate his own son the crowd flew into a rage and had Dr. Price arrested before the child's body had actually been burned.

    Dr. Price was charged with the cremating of a dead body, as the arresting police officers were convinced cremation was a crime.

However the police were not sure. At the trial Dr. Price defended himself and declared that while the law did not state that cremation was legal, it also did not state that it was illegal. The judge agreed, and Dr. Price was freed, and he was finally able to give his son a cremation which involved Dr. Price's own Druidic prayers. Dr. Price became famous over this incident and set the precedent that allowed cremation to eventually flourish in Great Britain.

In the United States <u>*Dr. Julius Lemoyne*</u> constructed a crematory in Washington, Pennsylvania which was constructed basically to cremate his own body upon his death, not for the public's use.

Regardless of politics, eccentricities, religious and philosophical resistance, by the turn of the 20th century cremation was again on the ascendency – as always happens history was repeating itself, and this present track of cremations ascendency still has not altered itself, but kindly recall the last time cremation fell out of favor that period lasted 1500 years, in our own time we have only seen the acceptance of cremation in contemporary life since the late 1800's historically speaking just a tiny piece of time only a little more than 100 years.

It is time for our last transition in our gray area of history: Cultural nuances that fiddle with death attitudes.

4. <u>CULTURAL NUANCES THAT FIDDLES WITH DEATH ATTITUDES:</u>

Cultures are from a consistency point of view somewhat fickle. Here is an example about the cultures fickle attitudes towards

28

cremation: first, cremation was popular for a couple of centuries, then cremation became unpopular for a whopping fifteen centuries, now cremation had become popular again for the last very brief historically speaking 100 years. Sounds fickle, well it is, and it is fickle because the pesky death rate being 100% and then add human beings to this inevitable mix and the result is that consistency of behavior and consistency in human attitudes flies right out the window. There can be no expectations of consistency, normalcy, or standards when we combine the myriad cultural aspects of death and add in cremation.

What is even more fascinating is that given all our fickle cultural behaviors, in the end each specific culture thinks and most importantly feels that the way they do things is the right way to do things. Sociologists call this "ethnocentrism" and ethnocentrism, (meaning the emotional attitude that my culture is the best) is alive and well when it comes to death rituals, and the choices people make concerning the ultimate disposition of their dead.

However for all our cultural diversity, historically one gold thread has united most cultures worldwide when the issue of physical death has been concerned, and that common thread was the mystery of death.

Throughout the history of death care a sense of true, verifiable, and authentic mystery has surrounded the death of another human being. For the most part our ancestors looked at the dead and felt strange feelings and sensations, they were filled with awe and reverence, and also fear, and hence many turned to religious thinking to explain what happened to us after we were dead. This mystery of death concept was a powerful and long lasting phenomenon which is still observed today, but things have changed and changed significantly concerning our basic attitudes towards, not cremation necessarily, but towards physical death, and particularly our own physical death, and towards the concept about a personalized individual mystery of death and hence embracing and learning lessons our ancestors were compelled to learn from the glaring 100% death rate that they most visibly had to confront most every day.

The mystery of death has motivated people to do all sorts of ritualistic activities which ranged from the simple to the bizarre over the centuries.

However the mystery of death has been in recent times slowly replaced by another attitude called the denial of death and this combined with several other factors have changed and will continue to change the history of cremation and the history of earth burial significantly.

Let us further and in more depth explore this notion of the mystery of death.

Over the historic time span that this chapter has been exploring the mystery of death was certainly a prevalent and familiar and constant companion for most of our ancestors and their attitude towards death. Over the ages of time the mystery of death propelled and motivated people to behave in certain ways, and to quickly and innocently accept certain ways of thinking as we have read about throughout this chapter. The mystery of death served as a powerful control mechanism and profound influence on how people thought and this control of thought came from the governments of nations, from religious organizations and from cultural mores and folkways for centuries.

For instance in teaching attitudes about the subject of the mystery of death the church historically was very clear. The church taught reverence concerning the dead was to be practiced in both thought and deed, and hence the important focal point of a funeral was not the mourner's grief but the symbolism and soul of the corpse. The church was also very clear on how people should think about death, the life hereafter, and what happens to a person after they are dead (heaven or hell).

In fact so powerful was the religious and cultural influences concerning the mystery of death for the ordinary person inhabiting the earth, the rituals and attitudes became set in stone, the prayers required for the transmigration of the soul were set in stone, and the body, the actual physical body had to be returned to the earth intact for the expectation of the literal bodily resurrection of the body. This thinking was set in stone and received powerful government support. Remember there was a time in history that if you cremated someone the punishment was death by the government.

The same accounts can be spelled out for political control and cultural demands concerning the mystery of death. In this or that country the government handles death this way, people comply and this is how things are done. For instance some cremations are controlled exclusively by the government, as are funerals and burials.

Culturally speaking, you cannot go five miles in any one direction on the earth where death and attitudes towards the mystery of death is handled in the same way, and even though funerals are deemed a cultural universal, every hamlet on the globe does them differently. The historic cultural response to the mystery of death has been profound. It takes only one visit to Westminster Abbey and a quick tour of the myriad of funerary architecture to verify the accuracy of this idea.

The history of cremation has generally over time been a history where the act of cremation itself ended up being an irritating and intolerable affront to the traditional thinking and cultural attitudes about the sacredness of the mystery of death.

However the history of viewing cremation as being irritating and intolerable has not lasted over time it has changed. The history of cremation has changed, and primary to this change is the cultures definite movement from deferring to the age old concept of the mystery of death to embracing the contemporary attitude of the individual's ability to deny the reality of death. This movement is so new, yet has already had consequences for humanity. However precisely what will be the outcome of such a cultural shift concerning death has yet to be written.

The utter power of the human's confrontation throughout history with the reality of the mystery of death gave rise to countless rituals and ceremonies that were viewed as inviolate. These rituals, throughout, could not be reformed, changed or altered. As it is with so many traditions, cultural mores, and folkways the customs seem to be judged on the basis of age and point of origin, and hence the mistaken assumption has frequently been made that the older something is, the better it is. Conversely it has many times been equally supposed that if something has its origins outside of one's own culture, or comfort level, or personal conviction, then whatever that is becomes inferior and unusable.

For 1500 years cremation fell under the category of the inferior, the intolerable and the unusable, but no longer. By the shifting of the cultural, religious, and governmental attitudes away from the mystery of death to a personal denial of death the methods of rituals, ceremonies, and disposition of the dead have been reformed, have been changed, and have been altered, hence the history concerning cremation is still being written.

What will they write about cremation? What will be said when historians look back at the history of cremation in say 1000 years from now, when yet another ten thousand attitudes have come and gone concerning disposition of the dead? Future historians may well attribute the contemporary acceptance and growing acceptance of cremation to the secular demythologization of the ancient approach to the mystery of death. In other words living people become totally immune to the issue of physical death. Is that a possibility?

It is odd and interesting that the denial of death (not others death, a denial of my death) is about as epidemic as it ever has been in history. It is clear that many cultures have succeeded in making death literally invisible (for example our cemeteries resemble golf courses). The mystery of death, ultimately symbolized throughout history by the corpse, has been replaced. The dead body has been supplanted by the experience, the celebration of the living, and by the extremely dangerous and risky modern idea that death really has nothing to do with the living. The corpse then becomes a nuisance, something to be gotten rid of so to speak and gotten rid of fast.

The further any culture distances itself from respecting and/or even being aware of the utter mystery of death and their ultimate connection to this reality, the closer that culture also begins to believe the meaningless idea that death has nothing to do with them.

When the mystery of death no longer fills people with awe or worse when the mystery of death is not even interesting or irritating, when the living replace the essentials of a death ritual (such as being around dead bodies, opened graves, witnessing the cremation) with the experiences of a party like socialization, then the lessons to be learned in confronting the mysteries of death easily become secondary or are entirely absent. When death essentials become secondary many other factors such as expediency, ease, simplicity, fast and invisible sweep into the death scene void. It seems the issue of identifying the essentials of a death experience comes down to recognizing through discernment and thought what indeed are the essentials which possess depth of thought as compared to the accessories of the death experience which might be shallow and hollow?

Let's explore this idea further. For instance, for the first time literally in the history of the human experience we live with some basic assumptions about life that we simply expect they almost appear as our birthright, but that the people before us and throughout history had no idea about, and if they ever even entertained such fantastic ideas about life and shared them they would have been easily declared mad.

Here are some cultural assumptions which certainly make up part of the attraction of cremation, and also certainly contribute to the demythologizing the mystery of death. For the first time in recorded history and this is particularly true in the West our life spans have extended themselves into age attainments that just 100 years people would have thought utterly unimaginable. For instance in the United States in 1900 the average man lived to be 43 years old, today the average life span is in the late seventies. This fact alone pushes the mystery of death further away than it ever has been in history because it is risky not to speculate and take great comfort in the notion that if I make it to 78, why not 85, then why not live to be 100? This type of life, extended life thinking sets up walls concerning one's own personal awareness of the reality of their own death – this is a form of the denial of death.

Compare this to the honest embracing of the mystery of death. The mystery of death approach says something quite different and honestly that if I am 78, 85, or 100 then I am honestly closer to my death than ever before, and hence I should feel the urgency to live my life to the fullest, to make amends, to say things that so desperately need to be said. This is the life affirming motivation that respecting and just being aware of the mystery of death has at its core.

Conversely the denial of our own personal death, underestimating the knowledge which is inherent in exploring the mystery of death makes people easily forget and abandon the wisdom lessons to be learned from exploration, but this takes time, and one contemporary observation is that many people do not wish to take time to discern and reflect, and make no mistake when this happens it affects our attitudes towards life, towards death, and hence when many people adopt this disconnect with death a new history is being written. What has just been explored also has had a tremendous effect on cremation.

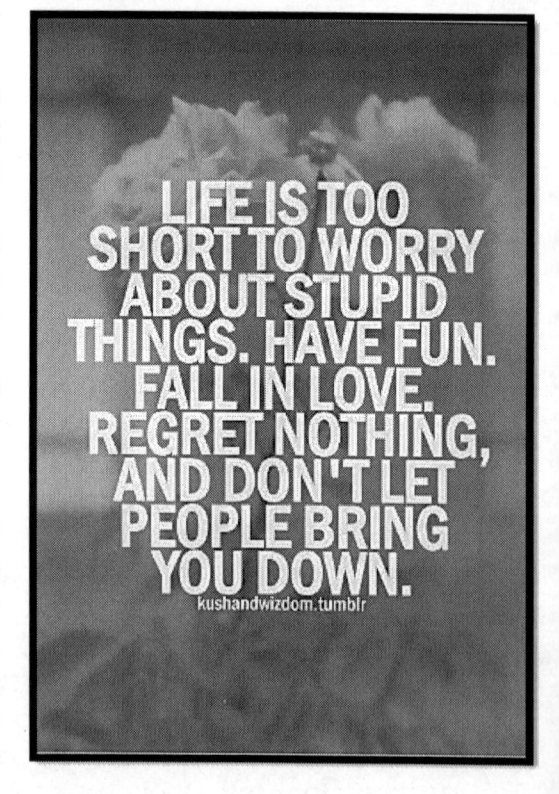

Add to this that we are today socialized to stay young, happy, carefree, wealthy, and sexy, and when this happens for thousands of people the mystery of death not only falls off people's consciousness, if it is even thought about, the subject of death becomes a nuisance, a bother, something to be ignored, a bummer, and hence a tremendous cultural collision is created because of one simple fact: no matter what the attitude is towards the mystery of death, the death rate is still 100%. Something to ponder, is it not?

The next cultural issue concerns the matter of immediate gratification, getting it done right now, no waiting, no thinking, no patience, no kindness and no bother. Said yet another way getting it done fast and just the way I want it.

Our history in death activities teaches us an extremely insightful and wise lesson and here it is: people everywhere on the face of the earth will care or not care for their dead based on the way they have lived their lives. Here is an example of living life: there was a time if you ordered a hamburger, French fries, and a beverage you had to wait 30 minutes and people waited. Today ask this question "Would anybody wait 30 minutes for a Number 4 at McDonalds?" The answer would be a firm no.

The concept of immediate gratification has also had a profound impact on the current history which is being written about cremation. Forget the mystery of death ponderings, cremation is attractive to many simply because it simply reflects how they have lived their entire lives – quick, easy, fast, convenient – and many times contemporary people are not even aware that their life has been devoured by such notions. In this environment the ponderous concepts of the mystery of death can still be found, but it is becoming increasingly rare.

Cremation because it reflects the way contemporary people live life in modern cultures namely – quick, easy, fast - can invade the deeper world of thought represented by the mystery of death, and replace it unwittingly with the denial of death. This certainly does not happen all the time, but it does happen, and it is happening more today than ever before in history. Cremation is not in and of itself a contributor to the demythologization of the mystery of death, and people's awareness of it – cremation however is clearly so much easier today than earth burial, and the consequences is that human beings seem to be wired to not think too deeply about something that does not come to them with great ease.

OTHER MOTIVATIONS FOR CREMATION:

Given all that has so far been said concerning history it is true that some people find they prefer cremation over earth burial for purely personal reasons – and their reasons are arrived at through careful thought and hence a conviction embracing cremation is arrived at. There have been no overt religious, governmental or cultural influences forcing this decision, the decision has been thought out, investigated independently and the conclusion for that person is that cremation is a wise choice. These people are not in the denial of death, they have confronted honest reality and they have selected cremation. They have embraced a mature attitude towards death, that affirms for them that death is universal, irreversible and inevitable, and these individuals with good solid information select cremation, and many times also these people implement highly creative cultural mourning practices and ritualistic activities, which includes an acknowledgement of the mysteries of death. This happens, but it takes time and effort and motivation – these types of learned informed convictions, most times, just don't simply happen.

Then too some people are highly concerned with financial matters (regardless of actual personal financial wealth or the lack of it), and view funeral expenses as too expensive, and for these people cremation can be an attractive alternative because generally speaking cremation is less expensive than earth burial.

Then also there are the people that make up the distinct movement to simplify life to return to the "good old days" so to speak. These people grow their own food, bake bread at home, they return to canning vegetables and putting up preserves, to home schooling their children, to basically return to a simple way of life. People who adhere to the simplification of life may easily view a traditional earth burial as an unneeded complication in their funeral experience and thus choose cremation to make their death services as simple as possible. However today with the ultrahigh technology of even the simplest cremation, and the highly sophisticated and expensive mechanical machines and buildings needed to house such contraptions necessary for cremation people who adhere to simplification in life are viewing cremation as being far from true simplicity.   These people who are attracted to simplification are today looking seriously at simple earth burials, and they have even chosen a name for this simple back to nature process they call it "Green Burials."

Still others are making cremation history by promoting concerns for the protection of our environment and the potential negative environmental impact, and promote and adhere to the notion that cremation might be preferable for environmental reasons. Burial is a known source of certain environment contaminants, with the casket many times being itself the major contaminant (although this too has improved and changed greatly over the years). However one of the main arguments which environmentalists raise concerns the literal burial space and how much is left on the globe for earth burials. Many people feel as if earth burial is taking up way too much of the earth's available real estate and hence are strong advocates for cremation.

While the concern for "abuse" and use of space for earth burials is laudable the historic facts tell quite a different story. One of the oldest cemeteries in the United States in located in Boston, Massachusetts, and the oldest date of death of a headstone in this cemetery is 1629. Where then are the people in Boston buried who died in 1628, or 1627? The citizens of Boston were certainly burying people in 1628, but today those old cemeteries which have long been abandoned and forgotten are part of possibly the foundation for some mammoth skyscraper in downtown Boston. We have said in this chapter that nothing lasts forever, well our cemeteries don't last forever either, they too die and go away. The idea then that if we keep burying the world will become a cemetery is not accurate. True some individual smaller countries have this as a concern, but globally this is simply overstated.

Another point concerning this abuse and use of grave space is this. There are five billion (give or take a million) people on the face of the earth. One thousand dead people can be buried on one acre of land in single grave spaces. This means that if 5 billion people all died simultaneously every human being on earth could be buried in a single grave space on 7812.50 square miles of land. This is about the size of Massachusetts and about 6 times the size of Rhode Island.

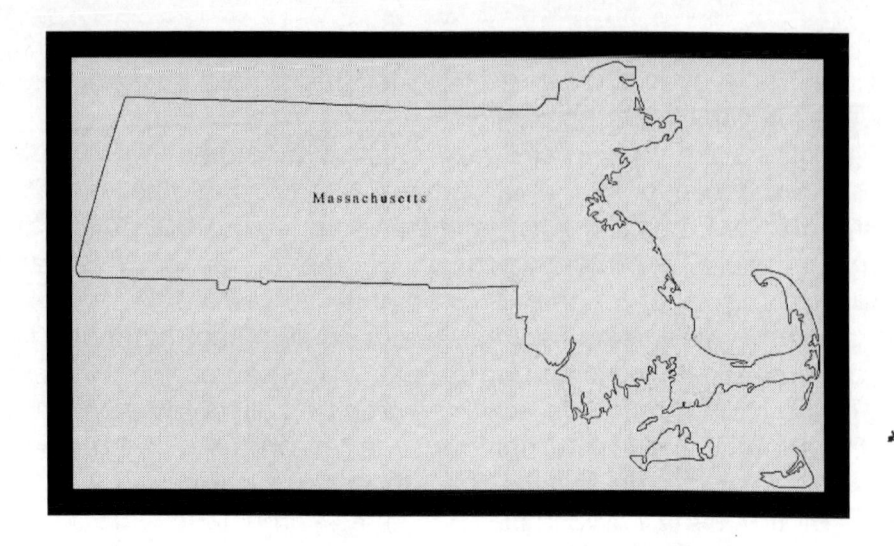

THE DOWN SIDE OF CREMATION

It seems to be in the vogue of things in many places across the globe to proclaim all the great and grand benefits of cremation, and to be sure there are many great and grand benefits as we have seen. However we need to be complete and examine that historically there have been and there are negatives to cremation.

We have already assessed the historical negatives that Judaism and Christianity had against cremation, and those negative feelings against cremation are still found in certain Jewish and Christian movements, although the prohibitions are clearly not as strong as they once were.

One common negative about cremation is the literal and utter permanency and destruction that happens in most every cremation. Dead bodies can be exhumed from a grave but dead bodies cannot be exhumed from a crematory chamber. Cremation is in fact highly and irrevocably destructive and once it is completed there are no other alternatives, even human DNA is completely destroyed. While this might not be a negative to the general public it has for years been viewed as a serious negative by law enforcement agencies such as the Coroner's Office and Medical Examiner's Offices, Police and Sheriff, who most generally take a dim view of cremation in general and of unauthorized cremations and of immediate cremations in particular for obvious medical-legal reasons. It is very difficult to do a forensic autopsy on a bowl of ashes and dust and bone fragments.

THE ULTIMATE DOWNSIDE OF CREMATION – THE RISK – THE RESULTS ARE PERMANENT

In early 2002, 334 corpses that were supposed to have been cremated in the previous few years at the Tri-State Crematory in the State of Georgia in America were found intact and decaying on the crematorium's grounds, having been dumped there by the crematorium's proprietor. Many of the corpses were decayed beyond identification, and horribly some families even had received cremated remains of their supposed loved one that were in reality made of wood chips and concrete dust.

Crematory operator *Ray Brent Marsh* had 787 criminal charges filed against him including theft by deception, abusing a corpse, burial service related fraud and giving false statements. On November 19, 2004, Mr. Marsh pleaded guilty to all charges and was sentenced to a 12 year prison term with credit for the time he had spent in custody before obtaining pretrial release on bond. He was also sentenced to 75 year probation following his incarceration. In actuality Mr. Marsh was facing a possible prison sentence of thousands of years.

Civil law suits were filed against the Marsh family as well as a number of funeral homes who had used the crematory services of Tri-State; these suits were ultimately settled. History has clearly proven that people need credible information about cremation and this leads to our next negative about cremation.

Another negative risk concerning cremation is the naïveté and general disinterest of the public concerning the blunt realities of the cremation process itself. The general public knows much more about the realities of what happens when a dead body is buried than when a dead body is burned up.

Many people in the public erroneously have the idea that cremation is clean, quick and easy. It may be quick and easy, but keeping it clean is difficult. The negatives of cremations, which the public is basically unaware of is the never ending issue of co-mingling of cremated remains, and the destructive nature of the cremation fire process itself. In fact many cremation contracts and authorization forms today state in very graphic descriptions in print the consequences of what a jet blast of fire blowing on a cadaver for several hours will do to the dead body. To some critics these graphic descriptions and blunt information seems uncaring and unfeeling for the bereaved yet from a legal position it is very understandable. Many attorneys have concluded that because of the basic ignorance and hence innocence of the typical cremation client as to what precisely goes on in the cremation process it is wise to spell out without any candy coating the realities of co-mingling, and spell out in detail just what happens to the dead body once the fire is ignited.

CONCLUSION

There is much activity going on in the cultures attitudes towards death, funeral, cremations and burials, and these attitudes are ever changing. Here our assessment of the present culture, with the demythologization of the mystery of death, our attempts to stay young, happy, carefree and wealthy, add to this our attraction to getting what we want done now with great ease, and then taking a long look at dysfunctional life styles, and what influence does organized religion have today as compared to 100 years ago. One can easily paint not a gray colored picture of historic transitions and traditions but instead a multi-colored modern art canvas which has colors running all over the place. This may well be one of the reasons that the history of cremation is changing so fast and as to why cremation has and is making a new and forceful presence in the beginning of the 21st century, but this trend will not last forever, it too will change, it is just a matter of time.

What do you think the historians will say about our cremation history and practices in 1500 years? It is a question worth discussion historically speaking of course.

THE STORY OF CREMATION AT A GLANCE

- Cremation practices can be traced to prehistoric and preliterate times.
- Burning of dead bodies probably began during the Stone Age (3000 B.C.) in Eastern Europe and the Near East.
- In the late Stone Age cremation began to spread across northern Europe.
- In the middle of the Bronze Age (2500 B.C. to 800 B.C.) cremation migrated to area throughout northern and western Europe.
- Around 1000 B.C. the Greeks used cremation as an integral part of the elaborate funeral customs. Both the poet's and historian's Pliny and Homer wrote about the prevalence of cremation in Greek culture.
- Early Romans copied the Greeks by adopting cremation around 600 B.C.
- In Rome during its Golden Age (27 B.C. – 395 A.D.) cremation was widely practiced.
- The practice of cremation was common with the Romans, but it had become a disliked subject with the Jews and early Christians. Cremation was considered it pagan.
- In 400 A.D. the Roman Empire by Constantine had completely eliminated cremation as a possible way to dispose of the dead.
- The historian Eusebius (263 A.D. – 339 A.D.) describes a Christian persecution in Lyon and afterwards the Romans cremated all the Christian martyrs as a way to mock the Christian's theology and belief in a literal bodily resurrection.
- In 217 the Roman Emperor Severus died and was cremated in York, England, and seven years later his cremains were returned to Rome.
- In 318 the authorities in Rome forbid burials and cremations to take place inside the walls of Rome.

- 789 A.D. Charlemagne (742 – 814) proclaims that any cremation is punishable by death for those who participate.
- 1300 – Pope Boniface (1235 – 1303) issues the statement that any Catholic who cremates or participates in cremation will be excommunicated.
- Pope Boniface also forbids human dissection. This began the formal protest position of the Roman Catholic Church against cremation and/or human dissection. The Church was firm concerning the human body being the temple of the Holy Spirit.
- 1409 – The first oven which can generate increased heat is invented.
- 1428 – Biblical translator John Wycliffe is exhumed and cremated 44 years after his death as punishment for his heresy.
- Sir Thomas Browne writes a book concerning funeral and cremation practices which is poorly received.
- 1710 the Treasurer of Ireland's wife requests publically that she be cremated upon her death, which created a political and religious scandal.
- 1826 – The first gas oven is invented.
- One of three Italian scientists and inventors Professor Brunetti perfected a model and displayed it at the 1873 Vienna Exposition.
- 1874 – Sir Henry Thompson (1820-1904), physician to Queen Victoria attends the Vienna Exposition and is intrigued by the cremation oven. Sir Henry eventually starts the Cremation Society of England.
- 1876 – Dr. Francis Julius Lemoyne builds for his own personal cremation the first crematory chamber in Washington, Pennsylvania
- 1878, The first crematory is opened in England at Woking.
- 1878 – The first German crematory opens in Gotha.

- The Welch eccentric Dr. William Price attempted to cremate his dead child by himself gets arrested and challenges the legality of cremation in England. The courts side with Dr. Price and his court decision opened up the ability for people in England to cremate their dead.
- 1884 – The first free standing public crematory is built in Lancaster, Pennsylvania.
- 1886 – Pope Leo XIII issues Canon Law 1203 which forbids cremation to Roman Catholics. Canon Law 1203 stated "The bodies of the faithful must be buried, cremation is forbidden as it denies the bodily resurrection."
- 1899 – *"The Modern Cremationist Magazine"* began publications.
- 1900 – Crematories spring up slowly throughout the United States and Great Britain.
- 1908 – The Catholic Encyclopedia refers to the practice of cremation as a "sinister movement."
- 1913 – Dr. Hugo Erichsen founded the Cremation of association of America.
- 1920 – The first Cremation Act was passed in the British Parliament.
- 1937 – The International Cremation Federation is founded.
- 1963 – Vatican II removes the strict prohibition against cremation. Canon Law 1203 is gone.
- 1969 – The Mungo Lady is discovered in Australia.
- 1975 – The Cremation Society of America changes its name to the Cremation Association of North American (CANA).
- 2002 – The Tri-State Crematory disaster occurs.
- 2004 – Ray Brent Marsh is sentenced to prison for the Tri-State disaster.
- 2015- The cremation rate continues to grow.

finis

Made in the USA
Columbia, SC
06 September 2024